Return of the
BUFFALO

WORDS BY **Jack Denton Scott**

PHOTOGRAPHS BY **Ozzie Sweet**

Return of the
BUFFALO

G. P. PUTNAM'S SONS · NEW YORK

Text copyright © 1976 by Jack Denton Scott
Photographs copyright © 1976 by Ozzie Sweet
All rights reserved. Published simultaneously in
Canada by Longman Canada Limited, Toronto.
PRINTED IN THE UNITED STATES OF AMERICA
Designed by Bobye List

Library of Congress Cataloging in Publication Data
Scott, Jack Denton, 1915-
Return of the buffalo.
1. Bison, American—Juvenile literature. [1. Bison] I. Title.
QL737.U53S36   599'.7358   76-19019
ISBN 0-399-20552-7   ISBN 0-399-61041-3 lib. bdg.

Second Impression

DREAMLIKE SHAPES drift out of the gauzy light of dawn, bringing to mind sights and sounds from the past: the war cries of Plains Indians; the defiant clatter of wagon trains as settlers pushed west; the rattle of gunfire; signal smoke smearing the sky.

Now, under a South Dakota sky as solid gray as slate, the shapes become real, and in their powerful presence these images from deep within the imagination dwindle and fade.

For here before our eyes are creatures that are a part of America's history like no other animal. The buffalo. They are living symbols of our heritage, dark shadows on our national conscience, stark reminders of the sometimes stirring, sometimes sad saga of a west that was won and then lost again to civilization's steady expansion.

Today there are two living species of these animals in North America: the plains buffalo of our story, which originally ranged over most of the country, except in the very arid areas in the Southwest and the Pacific coast, and the wood buffalo, larger and darker, which is found mostly in Canada.

But our most famous animal is not a true buffalo. It is a bison, called *Bison bison* by naturalists. However, we have been calling our bison "buffalo" for 300 years. It is believed that it got that name from early French explorers, who called it *boeuf*, meaning beef. English-speaking settlers made the French word buff, buffle, and finally buffalo. And it is as the buffalo, not the bison, that it thundered out of history.

Scientists claim that this largest wild animal of North America was alive during the end of the Pliocene epoch before the ice sheets slid out of the north and that about 25,000 years ago our buffalo came here from Asia across the Bering Strait land bridge.

The plains buffalo belongs to an old order Artiodactyla, of the family Bovidae, the same as *Bos taurus*, the domestic cow that gives us milk, butter, and cheese. That large bovine family also includes the Tibetan yak, the true Asian buffalo, goats, sheep, gazelles, and other even-toed hoofed wild ruminants with hollow unbranched horns always present on males and commonly on the females.

Today, unknown to many of us, these buffalo, once cruelly slaughtered to the brink of extinction and thought to be rare and a still-endangered species, have come bellowing to life again on ranchlands, prairies, and national parks.

Bearded, massive, these animals we are watching in the deceptive light of dawn are moving singly and in small groups to form a herd.

Buffalo do not move in one herd such as this one all of the
time. But they are gregarious animals and like to be with groups
of a dozen or so, although a herd sometimes swells to the
hundreds.

During much of the year the herds are made up of small groups consisting of females and young. This includes bulls up to four years old. Bulls over that age form their own group of about twelve that gather on the edge of the large "core" herds.

But throughout the summer, the rutting, or breeding, season, the bachelor bulls break up their groups, joining the females and the younger bulls.

During the mating season in July and August the buffalo are often restless. The entire herd is on edge. Even the usually placid cows are short-tempered and will fight one another.

During this period the big bulls challenge one another for dominance. Full-grown males try to depose bulls that have already gathered several cows into a harem. Others, just reaching the breeding age of three years, such as the ones we are watching, start with one cow.

Here two buffalo bulls stop grazing and swing their heads toward the same cow. The urge to mate attracts them slowly toward her as surely as if they were being yanked forward by an invisible lasso. That "lasso of love," as one poetic plainsman called it, soon pulls these two young males into a contest of superiority which starts with a bluffing game.

The two bulls first stand firm and glare at each other. If one bull isn't forced to walk away and look for another cow, then they will try nod threats, swinging their heads up and down in almost perfectly matched movements. During this maneuver the heads are raised most of the time. Attacks will come only when heads are lowered.

Both bulls now back off and stare at each other. Although they seem belligerent, both are cautious about combat. Because of fighting and breeding, the average mature male can lose as much as 300 pounds between June and October. Too many grueling fights would take off more weight and perhaps even weaken or slow down the breeding function.

Now the bulls try to outbellow each other, pawing the ground, tilting their muzzles upward and throwing out thunderous sounds.

At this point one of the bulls can give up without losing face. He will paw the ground and then lie down and roll and wallow. This, called displacement activity, is the respected way to decline the contest.

But both these young, untested bulls are determined to meet the challenge. They raise their tails high, lower their heads, and charge. The female, a two-year-old cow, which has just reached the breeding age, stands placidly watching.

Swiftly and surely, the bulls reach each other, crashing heads together with such force that one bull is almost knocked off his feet. The powerful impact is taken on the foreheads, not on the horns. Huge muscled necks absorb much of the shock of the charge. Sixteen-inch-long hair, growing thickly from the top of the head down onto the forehead, also cushions some of the crushing power of that impact. It is reported that the deflecting power of that hair is so great that a .30/06 rifle bullet fired into the hair from a distance of 30 feet did not penetrate the skull.

Suddenly, on the last charge, the slightly smaller bull staggers backward and nearly falls. They stand facing each other, breathing heavily, heads lowered. Slowly the beaten bull backs up, turns at a 180-degree angle, wheels around, and moves away. The winner takes several quick steps after him, then stops and watches him move off into the main herd. Battles can be bloody, for the buffalo's sharp horns can cut and gore, but rarely does death result from these contests.

The victorious bull goes and stands beside his prize. When he moves off to rejoin the herd, the cow follows him. In the days ahead this young bull will gather more cows into his "harem."

Zoologist Dr. Harvey L. Gunderson doesn't consider these cows to be in a real harem. He claims that among buffalo, as among domestic cattle, the male forms a tending bond with females in heat, but the bull leaves them shortly after they breed. The length of the tending bond varies from hours to several days. But one buffalo trait is certain: If the cows are receptive, the male will try to maintain that tending bond until all breeding is completed. This can mean a series of battles, some mini, some mighty.

Because it is the stronger bull that wins the contest and mates with a cow, not only is the survival of the fittest ensured, but a heritage of strength and vigor is passed on to his offspring.

The gestation period of the offspring varies from 270 to 285 days. This means a spring birth, with most of the young born in May.

As the time for the birth of the calves draws near, the bred cows stray from the main groups, gathering into their own groups of females.

The calf is born with the mother either standing or lying down. Most females lie in the prairie grass. At this time the female looks as if she were suffering from some severe skin ailment. Her shaggy coat seems to be peeling. It hangs in tatters. She is shedding her thick winter fur, but by the time her calf is weaned she will again have the normal sleek summer coat of the buffalo.

In sunlit flower-dappled grass the squirming wet calf is born with its eyes already open. It weighs from 30 to 70 pounds. It may be a soft brick red, a bright yellowish red, or sometimes a cinnamon color lightly tinged with yellow. Usually a single calf is dropped; rarely are there twins. Other females stand nearby to rush in and help protect the newborn calf if needed.

The birth, which is swift, has been timed at twenty-six minutes. This included the birth, the mother cleaning her calf and giving it the first nursing. But that mother was lying down, and the calf did not have to make the effort to stand and nurse.

Here the female carefully licks her newborn calf to dry it. Then she nudges it gently, urging it to its feet. It is weak, but willing, and makes many attempts to stand. It is usually about an hour after birth before the calf stands steadily and nurses, although some calves rise vigorously to their feet within a half hour and are following the mother around forty-five minutes after they are born.

Buffalo have less milk than domestic cattle, but it is more than twice as rich and very high in protein. A buffalo calf has to take only small amounts at a time to give it the strength and energy it needs.

In the next several days the calf rarely leaves its mother's side, nursing when it is hungry, patiently waiting while its mother grazes or raises a hoof to scratch her hide.

The female is very attentive to her calf. She watches it carefully, seldom moving more than a few yards from it, sometimes washing it or gently nudging it. She will defend the calf with her life if necessary. Observers have recorded instances where a female with a calf has held off wolves until help arrived from the herd. But she was so severely wounded by the wolf attacks that she died shortly afterward.

There is also protection in numbers, with several females and their calves remaining together until the young are strong enough and fast enough to move with the herd or with segments of it.

For days it seems that the calf is tied to its mother by an invisible string while she grazes or moves to the watering hole. It halfheartedly imitates its mother cropping grass, but it doesn't actually eat any.

Hours are spent lying down or just standing in the sun-warm grass. But after a few weeks, being a buffalo and a wanderer, the calf will scamper across the grasslands by itself in a bouncing lope, even approaching adult buffalo, tempting them to play and frolic with it. Some respond; some do not.

But the mother is never far behind, and soon she will turn
up to stand in proud possession beside her calf.

Two months after the calf's birth the hump begins to show, swelling slightly, growing rapidly from that time on. At that age a one-inch knob also appears on either side of the head, the horns to come. By midsummer the calf is weaned, but it will stay with its mother until the next spring, when at the birth of her new calf, it will leave her to join others of its own age.

If this calf is a male (and males have an edge, making up 54 percent of all calves born), it will become a mighty bull, said by many naturalists to be the most dangerous animal in North America, one that can easily defeat any natural predator except the huge and dangerous grizzly bear.

In eight years a male calf will look like this bull. When he is fully mature, his fur, a rich chocolate brown, shades to black in some places, and his black beard hangs from 8 to 12 inches. Standing 6 feet tall at the hump, weighing from 1,800 pounds to a ton, perhaps even touching 3,000 pounds, from 10 to 14 feet long, this bull in its prime can run 35 miles an hour, almost as fast as a racehorse for a short distance, and faster for long distances. Although bulky and clumsy in appearance, actually he is agile and surprisingly graceful. His normal life span averages twenty-five years, but he can live to be as old as forty.

The female we saw with her calf stands 5 feet tall and can weigh from 900 to 1,200 pounds. Buffalo experts believe that the female of the species is more intelligent, more courageous, and more vigilant than the bull.

The buffalo's senses are excellent. Hearing and smell are extremely keen, more effective than eyesight. Nevertheless, the dark-brown eyes of the buffalo can pick up the sight of friend or foe at two miles. Inner lips and tongue are blue-purple, with the tongue often flicking out to clean the nostrils, one quick flick into each nostril.

The buffalo is a grazing animal. The teeth in its upper jaw consist of three premolars and three molars on each side, no incisors or canines. The lower jaw has eight incisors in front, no canines, but three premolars and three molars on each side. This structure allows the buffalo to nibble and to grind grass easily. It is a ruminant, or cud chewer. It swallows grass only partly chewed and later, by regurgitation, brings it back into its mouth in small packs, or cuds, and takes its time to chew them more thoroughly into a soft, well-masticated mass. This well-chewed cud then passes through a unique stomach which contains four chambers—the rumen, reticulum, omasum, and abomasum.

The physical feature that makes the American buffalo a unique animal is the huge hump that rises behind its head like a strange growth. That hump is solid muscle. Hitched to extra-long shoulder spines, it gives leverage to lift the head, so huge and so heavy that even with the combined strength of hump hitched to those special shoulder spines, the head cannot be lifted above the level of the shoulder.

That hump also makes the hindquarters with its short, tasseled tail look too small to carry the weight of the rest of the body, giving a false impression that the rear of the buffalo is weak.

Hair also adds to that distortion of strength: Head, neck, fore part of body, and front legs are thickly matted with long hair, some of it well over a foot long. But the rear quarters are covered with short hair. Actually the buffalo is one solid unit of power, so strong it can upend an automobile with ease and smash down a heavy fence without apparent effort.

Crowning this powerhouse of hair and muscle are horns, which make an enraged buffalo so dangerous that when he charges, men have been seen dropping their rifles and fleeing in terror. With his hump and shoulder muscles, those horns become deadly stilettos that can rip, slash, and gore. Smooth as steel, sharp as a knife, the bull's horns are thicker and much larger than the female's. Short, thick at the base, tapering to a sharp point, they curve outward and upward from the sides of the head. Hollow, permanent, they are formed over a bone core that is an extension of the cranial frontal bone. Sizes vary with individuals. Some rise from the head like a pair of cutlasses. The largest on record had an outside spread of 35⅜ inches; the longer horn of the two was 23¼ inches along the outside curve.

Mighty as this plains animal is, he can be subdued by tiny creatures. Insects. In the spring, when the thick winter coat is beginning to tatter, exposing the animal's skin, hordes of insects are born which pester the buffalo throughout the summer.

To combat the biting insects, buffalo wallow. They prefer muddy places where they go down onto their knees, turn their heads onto the ground, then fall on their side, rolling onto their backs, then onto the other side. If lucky enough to find a mud wallow, that mud dries on the body, forming a coating that gives the buffalo a few hours' protection from the flies and mosquitoes.

If mud isn't available, then the besieged buffalo will find a dusty area to rub his head in, stretch out his body, roll vigorously, and do his utmost completely to cover and ease his itchy, bitten body with dust. The coating of dust helps keep off the insects. Standing in a strong breeze also wards off some insects, but nothing helps like the mud wallow.

Ten feet in diameter, saucer-shaped, a foot or more deep, the wallows are used constantly, preventing plant life from growing. They form permanent landmarks of buffalo country.

This prairie land still rich in knee-high grasslands has other physical features made long before the arrival of early peoples. It was land formed out of heat and cold, gouged into tropical swamplands, aswim in oceans and arctic ice, alive with the great prehistoric creatures such as the mammoths, some twenty times the size of the buffalo. These and other prehistoric creatures faced severe climate changes and catastrophes and lost, becoming extinct. But the buffalo survived and lived on to dominate the vast plains and prairie lands.

Their next enemy were the packs of wolves which the
buffalo also survived by using a special technique. Today on
the western plains there are buffalo rings, physical evidences
that tell us how the animals protected themselves and their
young from attacking wolf packs. Having an excellent sense of
smell, the cow matriarch would scent wolves and bellow a
warning to urge the segment of her herd into rapid motion,
the wolves in pursuit. The cows and calves gathered closely
together in an inner circle on a hillside, the bulls surrounding
them in a tight, close ring.

Circles were made as small as possible, so the fanged, darting wolves could not find a space between the bulls, their horned heads lowered. Sometimes these facedowns between buffalo and wolf lasted for several days. Observers report that the wolves seldom were the victors, so vigilant were the bulls. But if a buffalo stepped just a few feet out of the ring to do battle with a wolf, he was immediately dragged down.

As the buffalo stood and fought off the wolves, they pawed the ground and deposited their dung and urine. If the wolves were stubborn and the siege lasted for three or four days, the accumulation was considerable. After the wolves had left and the buffalo broke the ring and moved on, that area which had such a concentration of rich fertilizer grew grass that was taller, lusher, and greener than the surrounding vegetation. These striking green rings still mark those battlegrounds where the buffalo once held off the wolves.

Able to live on much less water than any other bovine, the buffalo also survived the severe droughts that blistered and cracked the land. Some died, but many lived.

And where there was water, the buffalo reveled in it. They became expert swimmers and used water to travel in, to drink, to bathe in, to cool themselves, to defeat insects. Entire herds have been seen swimming a river for a mile or more. It is not unusual for a buffalo to enter the water just for the enjoyment of a swim.

With their thick coats and hardiness, the buffalo has lived through blizzards that froze lesser animals. Always facing toward the storms, "pointing" it, they can raise their calves even in 40 degrees below zero.

Unlike domestic cattle, the buffalo does not paw through the snow to find grass. He uses his hairy head. Pushing his nose

into the snow, he swings his head from side to side, clearing
a path as effectively as a snow plow.

Long, fierce, extended storms and blizzards can fell even
the buffalo, but their strength and resistance are such that
many do survive even the most terrible winters.

The buffalo also had other living enemies to face in the past when it roamed the prairies freely. Friendly enemies. Indians. No one can say for certain how long the Plains Indians had lived in the land of the buffalo. But it is certain that they always admired and respected the animal with which they shared the land. They held the buffalo in almost as high esteem as they did their Great Spirit. He was called *Tatonka*, which meant next to God.

When the buffalo lived in the wild, it did not migrate in the true sense of the word. In the autumn there were large movements. The buffalo in the northern plains moved farther south in great herds. In the spring they reversed this movement. Always the wolves followed. So did the Indians. Often the tribes would erect their tepees and camp on the trail of the buffalo. The Indians were, in essence, caretakers of the buffalo herds, this country's first conservationists.

A single buffalo provided most items that a Plains Indian family needed to live. They used almost everything from the buffalo but its bellow. Even its beard decorated ceremonial costumes, bows, and lances. They drank its fresh blood, and the meat that wasn't barbecued, broiled, or stewed (methods believed to have been originated by the American Indian) was preserved in an ingenious way, later copied by the white man as a valuable survival food for armies and explorers.

Lean pieces of buffalo meat, usually the flanks, belly, and tougher portions, were cut into strips and sun-dried on poles. Then, with stone hammers, the Indian women pounded the meat into a paste. They converted it into pemmican by blending the meat paste with fat, herbs, and berries and pressed the mixture into small cakes. Lasting for months without spoiling, protein-rich pemmican sustained the Indians through food-short winter months and gave sustenance and energy without effort to hunters and braves on war parties.

Buffalo fat was used for tallow; its hair stuffed medicine balls; its ribs became arrowheads, dice, and scrapers. Leg bones were fashioned into knives, hammers, awls; hoes were made from shoulder blades. Skulls were used by the medicine men and as fetishes; hipbones became paintbrushes; horns were used as spoons, cups, and bowls. The tough buffalo sinews made bowstrings and strong backing for bows. Some slender bones were used as needles, special gouging tools, and musical instruments. Hides of the big bulls were worked into saddles, tepees,

and shields. Softer and smaller skins of the cows and calves were made into wearing apparel, robes, moccasins, and slings for the papooses. Buffalo hide was even stretched across a circular wooden frame to become a bullboat for crossing a river. Dried dung, buffalo chips, was collected and effectively used as fuel. The buffalo bladder was an excellent water bottle, its scrotum provided rattles for ceremonial dancers, and its tail became a whip or an insect swatter.

The Sioux, Crow, Kiowa, Apache, Cheyenne, Comanche, Dakota, Pawnee, Arapaho, and several other tribes' way of life was a definite buffalo culture. Their existence revolved completely around the unpredictable buffalo that could be in one place today and in another tomorrow.

The Indians prided themselves on the fact of life that although the herds were huge, they killed only the buffalo that they needed, were never wasteful, and did not hunt simply for sport. Their ways of harvesting the animals were unique and ingenious.

More than four hundred years ago, in 1541, the Plains Indians saw their first horses when Coronado and his soldiers rode into a tepee Wichita village. Future Spanish explorers and adventurers also brought horses. Many escaped and became wild, breeding on the plains. By 1750 the Indians had horses, and their way of life was completely altered.

Before that, however, they had had no means of transportation. Dogs pulled V-shaped frames with a section of net or wood upon which a load was carried. This travois was an advancement from the former primitive method of the dog pack and dragging loaded tent poles.

Hunting the buffalo was difficult and dangerous. With the Indians on foot and armed with stone-tipped lances and stone-tipped arrows, it was not easy to bring down the thick-hided,

agile animal, even though the hunters sometimes camouflaged themselves in buffalo skins to get close enough. Often the Indians would harvest them by stampeding, setting fire to the grass, and driving a segment of a herd past a line of archers, or a number of buffalo were herded over a high cliff. These buffalo "jumps" were clever operations, with Indians stationed strategically, spooking the lagging or cautious buffalo by shouting and waving robes and blankets.

They limited their kill to what they could use on the spot, carry back, and dry for later use. Any Indian who became overeager or too greedy in the hunt was punished by having his tepee burned and his possessions confiscated.

When they got the Spanish horses, the Indians continued to practice conservation, carefully selecting the animals they took out of the herds by riding close alongside and lancing the buffalo or shooting with an arrow. They never overkilled, even later when they used the effective surround system, where horsemen stampeded the buffalo into a circle and shot them from the edge of the herd.

The vast plains had room enough for the Indians and the buffalo. As far as the eye could see there were buffalo, there was grass, there was space—space for both the Indian and the buffalo to grow and to live in ecological harmony.

And then riding, walking, and in wagon trains came the harshest enemy of all. It had a devious name: immigration. Settlers left the eastern land of the new America to explore the west, to settle it, develop it.

Actually the earliest pioneers, like the Indians, saw the buffalo as a provider. It was a friendly and lifesaving animal that helped sustain them in the arduous push west across harsh, new, sometimes cruel land.

The buffalo provided them with meat and warm robes and guided them on their way. These early pioneers followed the trails the buffalo had trampled, thus avoiding too rough terrain and unfordable rivers. Those buffalo roads west that saved many a frustrating mile were described by Daniel Boone as marked in the earth "like the streets of a great city." Following those trails also led to water holes. When the snow piled high, buffalo were the bulldozers clearing the way.

In the beginning of the expansion west, the buffalo continued to thrive in the land that they still dominated. And dominate they did, with the greatest concentrations of animals that ever existed on earth. It has been recorded that not even the former millions of zebras, wildebeests, impalas, and antelopes of southern Africa could compare with the size of the American buffalo herds.

In 1871 soldier and historian Colonel Richard I. Dodge wrote: "From the top of Pawnee Rock I could see ten miles in almost every direction. This whole space was covered with buffalo, looking at a distance like a compact mass."

Colonel Dodge came down from Pawnee Rock and traveled for 25 miles along the Arkansas River in Kansas, moving with the herd that he had viewed (later estimated at 4,000,000 animals, 50 miles deep). It took five days to pass him at a given point.

Flat facts, without adjectives, tell what then happened to the world's greatest concentration of animals. Less than twenty years after Colonel Dodge saw that one gigantic herd, the buffalo in America, estimated by naturalist Ernest Thompson Seton (on the basis of total range, abundance in some regions, scarcity in others) at 60,000,000, were reduced to *541 animals*. This figure was totaled by naturalist-historian William T. Hornaday in his early and accurate *The American Natural History*.

This incredible carnage would have been accomplished even more quickly if the buffalo range hadn't been so large. It occupied about one-third of the continent, from Canada south to Mexico, with the bulk of the herds in the basins of the Mississippi, the Missouri, and the Ohio rivers. From that central region they ranged east to the Appalachians and beyond, west of the Rocky Mountains.

As expansion continued and grew, buffalo hunting became the main part of the business of the "winning of the west." Between 1873 and 1874, in Fort Worth, Texas, alone, sales of 100,000 buffalo hides were recorded every day. That figure is is astounding, but also consider that for every hide sold (from 75 cents to $2.50 apiece, depending on size and condition) about five hides were destroyed because of heat rot, careless skinning, and poor transportation. Meat couldn't be preserved, so mainly just the buffalo tongues were taken, salted, and sent east, where they sold as a delicacy for 50 cents apiece. Thousands upon thousands of buffalo carcasses rotted on the plains.

From 1872 to 1874 the Kansas Pacific, Omaha Pacific, and Santa Fe railroads shipped from the west 1,300,000 hides, 6,700,000 pounds of meat (mostly tongues and humps, also considered a delicacy), and 3,200,000 pounds of bones, used for fertilizer.

Sixteen hunters established a record by killing 28,000 buffalo in a single short summer. William F. Cody became "famous" and "Buffalo Bill" by killing more than 4,000 buffalo in seventeen months to feed the workers of the Kansas Pacific Railroad.

A few horrified Americans protested, but Congress refused to act. Finally, in 1874, a bill to protect the buffalo was introduced in the Texas legislature. But the popular Civil War hero Gerneral Philip Sheridan made an appearance before the legislature and declared that the buffalo actually were the commissary of our enemies, the Indians, and if we were to bring expansion and civilization to the west, both buffalo and Indian must be completely destroyed. The lawmakers agreed.

Half the remaining buffalo, most of the southern herd, about 4,500,000, were slain during that year (and the two previous years) while the Texas legislature dawdled. A lax Congress sat silently in Washington as we won the west by slaughter.

The few remaining wild buffalo were those that fled to the inaccessible high areas of Yellowstone National Park. Hunters followed them, but the plight of the last of the species finally got through to the government, and in 1894 Congress was prodded into passing a law prohibiting the hunting of buffalo in Yellowstone National Park. But it was not until 1902 that congressional action was taken actually to preserve the buffalo. Then Congress authorized the purchase of twenty-one animals from privately owned ranch stock to strengthen the Yellowstone herd.

But no law saved the buffalo.

It was a few compassionate and farsighted men.

We have the buffalo with us still because of Michel Pablo of Montana, Colonel Charles Goodnight of Texas, C. J. Jones of Wyoming, and Pete Dupree and James Philip of South Dakota, who guarded, fed, and helped propagate the pitifully few animals that were left. From "such a quantity of them that I do not know what to compare them with, except the fish in the sea" the American buffalo became the rarest animal on earth.

In his look to the future Pete Dupree's story is similar to the others. He was a South Dakota cowboy. Participating in the last big buffalo roundup in 1881 on the Grand River range, Dupree, long a respecter of the big shaggy beast, had a premonition. He captured five buffalo calves and took them to his ranch. During the years his herd doubled and tripled until when Dupree died there were fifty animals. There was a discussion and a contemplation of slaughtering those buffalo and selling them to settle his estate.

To prevent that, another rancher, James Philip, bought the buffalo and fenced them on his ranch north of Fort Pierre, South Dakota. By 1904 Philip's herd had grown to eighty-three. Buffalo experts believe that today nearly every living animal is descended from that Dupree-Philip herd.

In 1914 the state of South Dakota bought 25 buffalo from Philip and released them in Custer State Park. Now about 1,500 buffalo roam the park's 72,000 acres.

Even today South Dakota probably has the largest herds, most related to the Dupree-Philip buffalo. Wind Cave National Park has 350. Badlands National Monument has over 200. Ranchers in the state have several sizable herds, with Roy Houck's Triple U ranch in central South Dakota holding the world's largest private herd of more than 3,000 animals.

That there also are buffalo in our national parks and refuges today probably can be credited to naturalist Ernest H. Baynes, Dr. William Hornaday, then president of the New York Zoological Society, and Martin Garretson, who formed the long-defunct American Bison Society in 1905 and urged government action in preserving the buffalo for all Americans.

Herds can now be viewed in Yellowstone National Park in Wyoming, Montana, and Idaho, the National Bison Range in Montana, Wichita Mountains National Wildlife Refuge in Oklahoma, Fort Niobrara National Wildlife Refuge in Nebraska, Wind Cave National Monument, and Custer State Park in South Dakota. Canada also has them, with the largest herd of about 15,000 in Wood Buffalo National Park in Alberta.

But, again, it was individuals, not government, who distributed the buffalo in every state except fifteen, and one man, the aforementioned Roy Houck, in particular. He assembled a group that created the National Buffalo Association in 1966. It was dedicated to making the buffalo a permanent part of the American scene.

With 250 active members, 300 associate members, and 25 honorary members, the National Buffalo Association is helping in the propagation of buffalo in government-owned parks and refuges and is largely responsible for taking the buffalo off the endangered species list. Current buffalo population is about 40,000, with 5,000 in refuges and parks and another 5,000 owned by nonmembers of the association.

This may not seem like many buffalo. But where once, not long ago, there were only a half a thousand in the entire United States, there are now many herds, large and small. It is estimated by the National Buffalo Association that our herds will continue to grow by at least 5,000 animals every year.

We can finally feel secure that we will always have the animal that represents both the strength and the weakness of our country again roaming some of the land where it once was king.

When the dawn comes smoking up, mistily marking a new day in South Dakota, and the buffalo begin to move and the calves nurse on the vast ranch of Roy Houck, whose buffalo roam in this book, it seems certain that our national animal has indeed returned to us. Returned to stay. For perhaps we have learned a lesson from the buffalo.

To keep that lesson always before us, Mr. Houck, who was partially responsible for the dawn of the new day for the buffalo, reminds us of a part of the message Chief Seathl of the Duwamish Tribe of the state of Washington wrote to the President of the United States in 1855 regarding the proposed purchase of the tribe's land: